THE BEST OF 2017 SMARTIDEAS

A collection of insights from MarketSmart's blog that helps busy fundraisers generate more major and planned gifts at lower costs, in less time with fewer resources.

Greg Warner

Copyright © 2018 MarketSmart, LLC
All rights reserved.
ISBN:1987734734
ISBN-13: 9781987734737

DEDICATION

For my wife, Nessa, and my children
Madison and Landon.

ACKNOWLEDGMENTS

I would like to thank my staff at MarketSmart for their dedication, and most of all, believing in me and our mission.

TABLE OF CONTENTS

1 Introduction
Some People Find me Abrasive. Here's Why. 1

2 Copywriting, Email, and Word Choice
How to Ensure that Your Letter Signer will Sign Your
Fundraising Letter Even if he/she Doesn't Like It 5

Start Putting These Fundraising Words Everywhere Right Now 7

Here's Why You Should Remove the Word "Bequest"
From Your Vocabulary 9

Most Fundraisers Use Email the Wrong Way 10

3 Big Reasons Why Email Open Rates Don't Matter
(And What You Should Measure Instead). 11

What's Missing From Most Nonprofit Mission Statements. 13

3 General Fundraising
If Asking for Donations Makes You Uncomfortable, Read This Now!. . 17

Should Your CRM Include Photos of Each of Your Donors? 20

The 80-20 Rule is Dead!. 21

Almost Four Years Ago, I Declared:
"The Fundraising Pyramid is Dead!" 23

Finally Revealed, A Profile of the Ideal Major Gift Officer 24

7 Simple Ways to Engender Fondness Among Your Supporters
for Yourself and Your Nonprofit's Cause. 25

4 Forces Primarily Responsible for Making People Charitable 27

3 Simple Ways Fundraisers Can Improve their LinkedIn Profiles
to Land More Meetings and Raise More Money. 29

When it Comes to "Moves Management," Are you Concerned Too? . . 30

Is Shaming an Effective Fundraising Strategy? 33

You've Got Leads (Identified Major Donor Prospects)
But Are They 'Outreach-Ready'?. 37

SMARTIDEAS: THE BEST OF 2017

Donor Psychology: Do You Know What Really Makes
Your Supporters Feel Good?............................40

The Simplest and Most Effective 6-Step Major Gift and Planned
Gift Marketing Strategy Ever 42

Why Mistakes Are Awesome and What to do About Them 43

Top 10 Ways You Can Benefit From Conducting a Donor Survey....45

4 Engagement Fundraising

8 Simple Ideas to Involve Your Donors and Build
Deeper Connections...................................49

The 8 Core Components of Engagement Fundraising and
Why You Desperately Need Them 50

3 New Phrases/Concepts Engagement Fundraisers Need to Know....56

The 5 P's of Engagement Fundraising....................58

Engagement Fundraising in 7 Simple Bullet-Points 60

What Fundraisers Can Learn from Restaurants and Waiters.........61

5 Planned Giving

News Flash: Most of Your Supporters Don't Really
Want to be in Your Legacy Society.......................67

Count Legacy Gift Dollars, Not Promises 68

Here's Why When It Comes to Planned Gifts, It Isn't
Necessarily All About the Relationship......................71

How to Structure and Staff Your Planned Gift Shop
for the 21st Century..................................72

TABLE OF CONTENTS

6 Major Gifts

6 Major Donor Expectations You Simply Cannot Ignore 79

How Big is the Average Major Gift? 80

Why Your Wealthy Donors Love Donor Advised Funds and
Why You Should Care 82

3 Amazing Quotes from Major Donors 83

7 Guest Posts and Other People

3 Major Donor Myths Broken by Andrew Olsen 87

Are You Hunting Mice or Antelopes?
(Guest Post from T.J. McGovern) 88

Riddle: How do You Measure The Success (Or Failure)
of Your Planned Giving Program? 90

The 4 Levels of Donor Commitment According to Mal Warwick 94

Claire's 9 Ways to Get the Major Donor Visit 97

Why Oprah Winfrey Gives Money to Build Schools in Africa
(The 8 Components of Impactful Giving) 96

7 Great Old Quotes About Philanthropy 100

CHAPTER ONE:
Introduction

CHAPTER ONE: INTRODUCTION

Some People Find me Abrasive. Here's Why.

Recently I was told, "Greg, you are one strong cup of coffee." I like that. **Here's why I am the way I am:**

1. **I believe life is very, very short.** Both of my parents died in their 60's. One of my best friends died at 54. I am 48. I think the fundraising sector needs to change, now! I don't have time to wait. Today could be my last day. I have a tremendous sense of urgency.

I believe I need to get things done now! I guess that makes me a bit abrasive.

2. **Complacency is a prelude to disaster.** Our sector is failing to improve. That frustrates me tremendously. The fact that revenues from charitable gifts have been stuck at just 2% of GDP (gross domestic product) for over four decades is a crime. And it's not the donors' crime. It's ours. We need to take responsibility for this. Imagine how much good could be done if we helped the revenues from charitable gifts grow to just 2.5% of GDP! That could add almost another $100 billion to help others! The sector can't be complacent any longer.

I believe the sector must change now! I guess that makes me a bit abrasive.

3. **The technology for success already exists.** Technology is a game-changer. When it's leveraged properly, it can make almost anything more effective— including fundraising. For example, just look at how much more efficient Uber, Apple, Google, and others have made all of us. But the nonprofit sector has been slow to adopt new technologies and strategies even though doing so would increase giving, make donors happy and make fundraisers more effective. But too often I run into people in the sector that don't want to change. They don't want to adopt new ways of doing things.

SMARTIDEAS: THE BEST OF 2017

I believe nonprofit staff needs to embrace new technologies now! I guess that makes me a bit abrasive.

4. **Too often donors are treated very poorly.** Sometimes I wonder if lots of nonprofit staff might not be donating. Could the majority of them, perhaps, feel that they don't need to donate since they already work hard all day helping to make an impact? If that's the case, then it explains why so many nonprofits have such poor retention rates. It explains why so many lack donor-centricity. You can't be donor-centric if you don't know how it feels to be a donor, can you? The absence of donor-centricity leads to poor treatment of donors. I think that isn't right and isn't nice.

I believe nonprofit staff needs to treat their donors the same way they'd want to be treated! I guess that makes me a bit abrasive.

I'm frustrated.
Remember, I got into this because I was a pissed off donor. I wanted to figure out how to ensure that donors, like me, were treated better.
Less spray and pray marketing.
Less show up and throw up fundraising.
Less abuse of major donors and others.

I beg you, please don't misconstrue my frustration.
What some perceive as *abrasive* others perceive as *passion*.
I'm on a mission. My train is moving. Will you get aboard? I hope so!
If not, please get out of the way because this sector must change for the good of donors everywhere, for the good of the beneficiaries of your donors' gifts, for the good of the staff at your organization, and for the good of millions of organizations around the world.

Whew! Maybe I should switch to decaf.

CHAPTER TWO:
Copywriting, Email, and Word Choice

CHAPTER TWO: COPYWRITING, EMAIL, AND WORD CHOICE

HOW TO ENSURE THAT YOUR LETTER SIGNER WILL SIGN YOUR FUNDRAISING LETTER EVEN IF HE/SHE DOESN'T LIKE IT

I'll skip to the end and tell you how: Set some ground rules with whoever you ask to sign your fundraising letter.

Usually, a letter signer won't sign a fundraising letter for the following reasons:
 a. Because it doesn't sound like her
 b. Because it looks weird (i.e. the letter is long, has too many underlines, funky bold lettering, etc.)
 c. Because it sounds too informal and colloquial

To ensure that your signer will sign the letter you've got to politely set some ground rules as follows:

GROUND RULE #1: It isn't about the signer. Explain that, when it comes to fundraising, the donor needs to be the hero and the signer needs to help make the donor feel that way. Therefore, it might not sound like the signer, it might not look pretty and the signer will probably think it won't work to raise money.

GROUND RULE #2: The signer's role. Her role is to sign the letter while yours is to do what you must to ensure that the letter does what it's supposed to do— raise a ton of money. Note: That's a polite way of saying that the signer needs to let you do your job. You have the expertise. This is what you get paid for. I know it sounds snarky but maybe you can make a deal with your signer as follows: You won't go to her office and try to do her job if she'll let you do yours (Be sure to smile when you say it).

GROUND RULE #3: This is a science. Fundraising letters are not like business letters, thank you letters, subpoena letters or any other letters. Tons of research has been focused on what works and what doesn't. Therefore, you need to make sure she knows that we don't "wing it" when it comes to writing fundraising letters. Her gut feel has not been tested (unlike your direct mail experience).

SMARTIDEAS: THE BEST OF 2017

GROUND RULE #4: You have the right to change signers. Whew! This one might be tough. But, you should seek to gain agreement in advance that the signer will let you switch signers if he or she doesn't like your letter.

CHAPTER TWO: COPYWRITING, EMAIL, AND WORD CHOICE

START PUTTING THESE FUNDRAISING WORDS EVERYWHERE RIGHT NOW

The words are listed down at the bottom. But to understand why you should put them everywhere, read this:

Every single one of your supporters wants to have a meaningful life and wants to be remembered fondly after their lifetime.

Many of these same supporters will contemplate the creation of or revision to an estate plan. And, every time they do, your organization has a big opportunity to acquire a gift. But how do you know when the opportunity has arisen? That's the big question, isn't it?

Here are some of the many life events that trigger this kind of thinking:
- Birth of a child, grandchild, niece or nephew
- Death of a family member or friend
- Illness or injury of a family member or friend (or themselves)
- Weddings or divorces
- Injuries, sicknesses and diagnoses
- Even hearing about a friend's estate causing lots of problems for others— such as their children
- And any other major events

People might even consider a gift at the precise moment when they are:
- Opening a new financial account
- Buying or selling securities
- Purchasing or revising a life insurance policy
- Buying real estate
- Selling a business
- Looking at items they own and want to "hand down" such as jewelry or furniture
- Viewing old photographs or videos (especially if they somehow relate to your cause)
- Getting a call from an old friend or long-lost family member
- Writing memoirs

SMARTIDEAS: THE BEST OF 2017

Because of every bullet-point listed above, your planned and major gift marketing needs to be ever-present and ubiquitous but at a low cost— not an easy task. Here's the easiest way to accomplish this. Put the following words everywhere you possibly can:

"Please consider making a gift to {your organization} in your will and financial plan."

- on emails;
- business cards;
- letterhead;
- mailers;
- reply forms;
- booklets;
- magazines;
- articles;
- photos;
- banners;
- invitations;
- research reports;
- website pages, etc.

CHAPTER TWO: COPYWRITING, EMAIL, AND WORD CHOICE

HERE'S WHY YOU SHOULD REMOVE THE WORD "BEQUEST" FROM YOUR VOCABULARY

The word bequest sucks when it comes to generating planned gift revenue. Stop using it. Here's why:

1. No one uses this word with their family and friends so you shouldn't use it with your donors… they won't "get it"
2. It reminds people about death and nothing scares people away from making planned giving decisions faster than thoughts about death
3. Dr. Russell James' research found that it increases the likelihood that donors will never be interested in a planned gift and decreases their interest in considering a planned gift as an option for supporting your mission

MOST FUNDRAISERS USE EMAIL THE WRONG WAY

Every marketing channel needs to be optimized and employed properly. Sadly, most fundraisers are using email the wrong way. Email should NOT be used primarily for fundraising. Rather, it should be used mostly to build engagement.

It should be used to **tell stories, involve supporters, report back how gifts were used and make them feel good**... not so much for asking.

Think of an email to a donor as you would an email to your friend. Would you only ask for money from a friend in every email? No, of course not. Maybe every once in a while. But you would do that sparingly and only when the time is right.

I wish fundraisers would finally learn to stop "blasting" and "start engaging." Too many treat email like the button they press to get money out of an ATM. That's not how it works. That's not how donors want to be treated.

It CAN be used to raise money. But donors first need to get value. If fundraisers would provide more value in their emails, they'll get more donations. If you give, you'll get.

One would think people employed in the 'charitable sector' would understand the law of reciprocity. Nonprofits need to **give first in order to grow their relationships with supporters** to the point where they feel that they got so much value that they absolutely MUST give back.

CHAPTER TWO: COPYWRITING, EMAIL, AND WORD CHOICE

3 BIG REASONS WHY EMAIL OPEN RATES DON'T MATTER (AND WHAT YOU SHOULD MEASURE INSTEAD)

First, a short story.

Recently, I participated in a roundtable discussion led by a salesperson for one of those cookie-cutter planned giving website companies. She was showing off her firm's marketing emails. As she presented her Powerpoint slides, she kept emphasizing how wonderful the open rates were.

17% open rate. 28% open rate. 34% open rate.

"Oooh. Aaah. Wow" said the others seated beside me.

Then I asked, "Why are you measuring open rates? They don't account for the effectiveness (or ineffectiveness) of email marketing. No smart marketer cares about them. I don't get it. Why do you keep talking about open rates?"

Stunned! The sales rep was stunned. She had no idea what to say. That's because she didn't know a darn thing about effective marketing. She was just spewing misinformation. Sadly, that's what I see happen at most fundraising conferences. That's why I rarely go to them.

Some people call email open rates empty metrics. Others say they are just a vanity metric. I'm here to tell you that there's simply no good reason whatsoever to measure them. Here's why:
1. Most email programs that block images misreport open rates;
2. Many opens on mobile devices such as Blackberry devices do not report that the email was opened;
3. And, finally, emails read in preview panes are usually not reported as opened.

So what should you measure instead?
- Clicks
- Number of pages visited

- Types of pages visited online
- Time on site
- Forwards/shares
- Shares on social media
- Inbound requests for more information
- Inbound phone calls

What really matters is engagement! Email open rates are faulty and useless!

So the next time you hear one of those cookie-cutter planned giving website salespeople tell you about their open rates, tell 'em you know better.

CHAPTER TWO: COPYWRITING, EMAIL, AND WORD CHOICE

WHAT'S MISSING FROM MOST NONPROFIT MISSION STATEMENTS

Everything I think, write and create begins with the donor in mind — not the fundraiser. Sorry. I guess it's because I think "donor-centricity" is a term that's tossed around a lot but isn't truly applied properly enough.

Keep in mind, I started this business and invented our technology because I'm a pissed-off donor.

I want fundraisers to focus on me, not my transactions. I want them to understand why I care and how I want to find meaning in my life more than understanding how to get myself a tax deduction.

Take a look at the following mission statements and see if you can guess what's missing.

- **American Diabetes Association:** To prevent and cure diabetes and improve the lives of all people affected by diabetes.[1]

- **American Cancer Society:** The American Cancer Society is the nationwide community-based voluntary health organization dedicated to eliminating cancer as a major health problem by preventing cancer, saving lives, and diminishing suffering from cancer, through research, education, advocacy, and service. No matter who you are, we can help. Contact us anytime, day or night, for information and support.[2]

- **World Vision:** World Vision is an international partnership of Christians whose mission is to follow our Lord and Savior Jesus Christ in working with the poor and oppressed to promote human transformation, seek justice, and bear witness to the good news of the Kingdom of God.[3]

Did you figure out what's missing?

---

1 http://www.diabetes.org/?referrer=https://www.google.com/
2 http://relay.acsevents.org/site/DocServer/Mission%20value%20Sheet.pdf?docID=81060
3 https://www.worldvision.org/about-us/mission-statement

SMARTIDEAS: THE BEST OF 2017

The donor!

Fascinating, isn't it? In fact, search mightily. You'll be hard-pressed to find a charity mission statement that includes their donors — the very people that provide the funding to fulfill each charity's mission. The people who work hard their entire lives, then give away their hard-earned dollars. The people who care so deeply they give until it hurts and sometimes lessen their own children's inheritances to make room for their beloved charities.

Is it me or is something wrong with the fact that nonprofit mission statements fail to include the people that make it all possible?

I'm thinking this is exactly why donor retention rates among nonprofits are in the toilet. How on earth can nonprofits expect to have high donor retention rates if they don't even include their donors — their needs and their desires to find meaning in their lives — in the mission statement?

What do you think? Should donors be included in nonprofit mission statements?

P.S. – In case you're wondering, yes… *nonprofits* are mentioned in my firm's mission statement. So are supporters.

CHAPTER THREE:
General Fundraising

CHAPTER THREE: GENERAL FUNDRAISING

IF ASKING FOR DONATIONS MAKES YOU UNCOMFORTABLE, READ THIS NOW!

Recently I was asked the following: "The whole idea of the 'ask' is very uncomfortable to me. How can I become more comfortable with it?" Here's my answer:

First, if you are uncomfortable with asking, it's probably for one or all of three reasons.

1. You don't passionately believe in your organization's mission and its ability to accomplish great things with donations.
2. Your donor is not ready to be asked.
3. You are in the wrong position and should not be "asking."

I'll go into each of these three first. Then I'll answer the big question, "How can I become more comfortable with it?"

1 - No passion.

I hate to be crass (actually, that's a lie… I love to be crass), but if you are not passionate about your organization and its mission, you have no business asking people to give to support it. Don't tell me you need the job to support your family, pay your bills or repay your education loans. I don't care because I don't think it's fair. Donors deserve engagements with fundraisers that are just as passionate about the cause as they are. Giving via a fundraiser who doesn't really care about the cause is like buying a car from a huckster. You can't fake passion. If you try, the donors will sense it and you will fail to reach your fundraising goals anyway. Then, nobody wins.

2 - They aren't ready.

Although the Mongols defeated Korea and (much bigger) China, they got hit with typhoons both times they tried to invade Japan. Because of bad timing, they failed. Similarly, if you ask for a donation when the time is wrong, you probably won't succeed. When it comes to 'asking,' timing is important. You need to know if your supporter is ready. Is their passion high? Have their questions been answered? Do they have good reason to give? If the answer to these questions is "no," the timing might be wrong and your sense of it will make you feel uncomfortable for good reason.

3- Wrong position.

Do you enjoy talking to people and learning about them? Do you like to make people happy?

More importantly, do you have hang-ups with regard to talking to wealthy individuals? Do they make you uncomfortable because you can't get past the fact that they have a lot of money? Does their wealth make it hard for you to see them as human beings with needs, dreams, and passions? Most people won't want to admit that they have these kinds of hang-ups. But, make no mistake, they exist for a lot of people. And, if they exist deep within you, then you might be in the wrong position. You can't fake your way through this job. So don't try.

Now, if you do have a bona fide passion for your cause, if your donor is ready, and if you are in the right position, here's how you can be more comfortable with asking:

1 - **Think of yourself as a facilitator, not a fundraiser.** Realize that your job is to help people achieve their goals. You aren't taking money from them. You are giving them an opportunity to find meaning in their lives and feel good. Think of it that way and you'll become more comfortable asking.

2 - **Think of yourself as a matchmaker, not a fundraiser.** Your job is to align programs and organizational needs that help your nonprofit's beneficiaries with people who have passion for those programs and needs in addition to having the capability to make a tremendous impact. Your job is to be a matchmaker. Think of it that way and you'll become more comfortable asking for donations.

CHAPTER THREE: GENERAL FUNDRAISING

3 - **Think of yourself as a service person, not a fundraiser.** Your job is to serve the donor. You should be spending time making sure you know what's going on so you can convey information properly. You should also be putting forth effort to get to know your donors' needs. Then you should be spending time communicating relevant information that aligns with each donor's needs. Furthermore, you should help your donors move themselves through the consideration process. Service is the key. It isn't about asking, it's about serving.

SHOULD YOUR CRM INCLUDE PHOTOS OF EACH OF YOUR DONORS?

My uncle is a radiologist. Recently he told me about a 2007 study of radiologists.[4] The study found that including a photo of a patient along with their imaging exam results made doctors more successful.

Here are the results from the study:
1. The imaging exam results with photos of the patients resulted in more meticulous readings from the doctors interpreting the images leading to 80% more incidental findings of unexpected abnormalities that had health implications beyond the scope of the original exam. In other words, the photos caused the doctors to look more carefully at the results of the exams without necessarily spending any more time on their reviews. The more careful reviews led to more unexpected findings of more medical issues that needed to be treated.

2. Furthermore, 100% of the radiologists tested admitted feeling more empathy toward the patients.

After I read this I began to wonder if, perhaps, fundraising CRM should include photos of each donor by syncing with open API's that social media like Facebook, LinkedIn and Twitter provide.

Wouldn't that increase donor empathy, donor-centricity, and overall fundraising effectiveness?

What do you think?

---

[4] https://www.sciencedaily.com/releases/2008/12/081202080809.htm

CHAPTER THREE: GENERAL FUNDRAISING

THE 80-20 RULE IS DEAD!

76/10, not 80/20!

Last year the Congressional Budget Office released a report[5] about wealth in the United States. Here are some points to consider:

- The top 10% of families held 76% of total wealth in the U.S.
- The average was $4 million net among the top 10% of families after paying off debts
- The bottom 51st to 90th percent accounted for only 23% of total wealth
- The entire bottom 50% of the U.S. population holds just 1% of the wealth in the U.S.

This backs up another report that found that 44% of Americans live in "asset poverty" with just 3 months' worth of savings. In other words, you can stop targeting almost half of the people in America with your fundraising efforts.

It also means that the 80-20 Rule is dead. I guess now it should be called the 76-10 Rule.

Where are you focusing your acquisition and retention efforts?

If your plan is to move people up the pyramid, you'll have a hell of a hard time doing that with people in the bottom 50% (with no liquidity or assets).

Here's an idea: aim to acquire people with wealth!

Then, once you acquire those new WEALTHY donors, survey them to determine:
- If they really have assets (and wealth)
- How old they are
- If they are highly educated

---

[5] https://www.cbo.gov/sites/default/files/114th-congress-2015-2016/reports/51846-familywealth.pdf

- Whether or not they have a donor-advised fund or family foundation
- Why they care
- Who inspired them to be concerned about your mission
- What assets would they like to give
- How would they like to give them away
- And more

It ain't rocket science.

The amazing thing is that the wealthy want to build a relationship with you and your organization. They want to give. But you have to understand who they are and what motivates them first. Then you need to cultivate the relationship with personalized, relevant, highly contextual communications.

CHAPTER THREE: GENERAL FUNDRAISING

ALMOST FOUR YEARS AGO, I DECLARED: "THE FUNDRAISING PYRAMID IS DEAD!"

Recently I was reminded of a blog post I wrote four years ago about the fundraising pyramid that got a lot of attention. (You can read it here: https://imarketsmart.com/the-fundraising-pyramid-is-dead/)

Some of the reactions were not so kind. Here's what some said about the blog article I wrote back then:

"Your assertions demonstrate that you clearly ARE from outside the fundraising world."

"It seems that you are confused about what "planned giving" means."

"I would say 99% of non-profit staff cannot "plan gifts" for an organization. Unless they happen to have one too many fully funded retirement plans that they would like to leave behind to lower the burden of inheritance tax on their children."

"I would submit that there are a lot of development people out there who could fill you in on the inaccuracy of your statement. And by the way, fundraising is not a subset of anything.

FINALLY REVEALED, A PROFILE OF THE IDEAL MAJOR GIFT OFFICER

Thanks to the Education Advisory Board[6], we now know what the ideal major gift officer looks like.

Their Advancement Forum sought to understand what makes a top major gift officer tick. So they surveyed over 1,200 major gift officers at 89 colleges and universities in the U.S.A and the United Kingdom.

According to their study, the ideal MGO is a "Curious Chameleon." They possess:
- Behavioral and linguistic flexibility
- Intellectual and social curiosity
- The skill to distill information
- The ability to be strategic

Sadly, these very successful Curious Chameleons make up just 3.8% of the MGO population (yet they have a 78% higher chance of exceeding their goals).

---

6 https://www.eab.com/research-and-insights/advancement-forum/infographics/inside-the-mind-of-a-curious-chameleon

CHAPTER THREE: GENERAL FUNDRAISING

7 SIMPLE WAYS TO ENGENDER FONDNESS AMONG YOUR SUPPORTERS FOR YOURSELF AND YOUR NONPROFIT'S CAUSE

People are more likely to be persuaded by people we like.

So, no matter how worthy your cause is, if your supporters don't like you, they won't make major and planned gifts to your employer.

Here are 7 simple ways to engender fondness for you and your nonprofit's cause:

1. **Be a chameleon** – In other words, take the time and put forth the energy to look the part. If you work at a University and your donors love the football team, hopefully, you do too. Even if you didn't graduate from the same school, wear their colors, put the team pin on your lapel and throw a bumper sticker on your car. If instead your employer's cause is to help improve the environment and its donors wear khakis and t-shirts, you should do the same. Showing up in a formal suit with shiny black shoes will only make them feel uncomfortable. Fundraising chameleons hearten trust.
2. **Use the law of reciprocity** – First, know that the most successful salespeople, customer services representatives, account managers and, of course, fundraisers genuinely like people and are good at making people feel liked. They know that their recommendations and proposals will be appreciated, evaluated and taken seriously if their recipients feel that they are coming from someone who likes them and is looking out for their best interests. Among the easiest ways to signal to people that you like them is to give them something. Pay them compliments, say their name aloud, or bring them gifts they'll enjoy. Whatever your tactic, make sure it's genuine. Don't try to con your donors. You can't fake liking. If you try to fake your giving, you'll be exposed and rejected.
3. **Be cooperative** – Fundraising needs to be a win-win. So it's important that you cooperate with your donors to help them achieve their goals. Then, and only then, you will achieve yours. Napoleon Hill, author of the best-selling book Think and Grow Rich said it best, "You can succeed

best and quickest by helping others to succeed."

4. **Be familiar** – Your donors might meet you but forget they did. Then they'll meet you again, and forget again. Don't be dismayed. They're busy. And besides, it's not their job to remember you. But it is your job to remember them and to make sure you become familiar to them. Why not include your picture on your website? Also, maybe you should consider including it at the bottom of your emails below your signature. If you do it right, familiarity won't breed contempt, it will help you raise money.

5. **Show 'em that you know 'em** – As a direct marketer for the past 25 years in the Washington, DC area I came to know Cal Sutphin, the co-owner of Braden Sutphin Ink Company. Everyone knew Cal and he knew everyone. He was famous for two things. He always wore a red tie and he remembered everything about everyone in the region. When he passed by he'd always say hello to me, "Hello Greg." But he wouldn't stop there. He'd ask, "How's Nessa and the kids, Landon and Madison?" Then he'd continue by asking, "Madi must be in middle school, right? How's she liking the change?" He was amazing; he was loved by everyone. And he sold a lot of ink! Then, after he retired in 2013 he wrote a book titled Red Tie's History of the Printing Industry that includes the names of 9,120 prominent people from the industry; 1,554 companies; 363 stories from people he interviewed; and 591 photos. Whether it's done face-to-face or via communication channels like email, remembering small details about people, makes them feel special. Be like Cal. Show 'em that you know 'em.

6. **Smile more** – Smiling implies warmth and happiness. Of course, donors like to be around people who are warm and happy. Smiling can actually improve your mood, too. Plus, you have been granted an unlimited number of smiles so you can give them away for free. So, smile more and you'll feel good. Plus you'll make your supporters feel good too.

7. **Listen…a lot** – When I was a kid, I was told that all of us were given two ears and one mouth and we were to use them to listen at least twice as much as we speak. If you listen a lot with the intention of learning, not as you merely wait your turn to reply, you'll help your donors show you the way forward. Focus on them. Let them tell you how they feel and what they want. Only by doing so will you have a chance at matching up their interests with programs that need funding.

CHAPTER THREE: GENERAL FUNDRAISING

4 FORCES PRIMARILY RESPONSIBLE FOR MAKING PEOPLE CHARITABLE

According to the author of a book titled **WHO REALLY CARES, Arthur C. Brooks,** there are **4 forces in American life that are primarily responsible for making people charitable:**

1. **Religion**
2. **Skepticism about the government's involvement in people's economic lives**
3. **Strong families**
4. **Individual entrepreneurism**

(NOTE: He's the president of the right-leaning think tank, the American Enterprise Institute. Some people believe his research was seriously flawed. I'll let you decide.)

Here's why (according to Brooks'):

1. **Religion** – People who pray every day (regardless of whether or not they go to church or another place) are 30% more likely to give money to charity than people who never pray. Simply belonging to a congregation— whether one attends or not— makes a person 32% more likely to give. People who say they "spend a great deal of effort" to their spiritual lives are 42% more likely than those devoting "no effort." People who say "beliefs don't matter as long as you are a good person" are dramatically less likely to give to charity and to volunteer compared with people who do believe that "beliefs matter." Nineteen of the twenty-five states with the fewest houses of worship per capita were below the national average in all types of household giving.

2. **Skepticism about the government's involvement in people's economic lives** – Brooks wrote that politicians and a significant number of people take credit for being charitable without spending their own money because they, instead, support policies of income distribution through taxation and this affects their private giving.

27

The result? Between 1933 and 1939, as spending to aid the needy went from zero to more than 4% of GDP, researchers concluded that government funds were directly responsible for nearly all the drop in church charity. Another study in 1985 came to the same conclusion. Other data shows that decreases in state funding stimulate charity. For instance, in the 1980's when President Ronald Reagan cut spending on social programs, charitable giving rose by 1/3. That point was surprising to me. A real head-scratcher!

3. **Strong families** – He wrote that "people who have children are more charitable than people who don't. Given that children are expensive and time-consuming it is surprising that parents make available more of their time and more of their money than non-parents. Generous parents make for generous kids. The question for most parents is how best to teach generosity to their children. Also, married adults (especially with children) give and volunteer at far higher rates than those who are single or divorced. So, single parenthood is a disaster for charity (21% less likely to give to charity than singles without children and 26 percentage points less likely to give) even if they have the same income, education, religion, and so on." Although other research has found that childless bequestors give much more in their after-lifetime donations. Nonetheless, could broken homes and poor parenting result in less charity?

4. **Individual entrepreneurism** – Brooks doesn't go into this as deeply as the other components but he does remind us that entrepreneurs are among the most charitable people in society. Of course, that makes sense because they have a lot of money. But apparently, it also makes them more charitable.

Putting aside his political agenda, I thought it was a worthwhile read.

CHAPTER THREE: GENERAL FUNDRAISING

3 SIMPLE WAYS FUNDRAISERS CAN IMPROVE THEIR LINKEDIN PROFILES TO LAND MORE MEETINGS AND RAISE MORE MONEY

Most fundraisers' LinkedIn profiles are screwed up!

They look like resumes, not invitations. After all, are you trying to raise money or are you looking for another job?

If you are aiming to raise money then you need to recognize that, more and more, your donors will check you out online before they accept your telephone call or email outreach. Then, if you land an appointment/meeting, they'll check you out again.

So what does your LinkedIn profile look like?

Is it written and designed to help you generate more donations or to help you get a job? If it's the latter, I've got a problem with that and so will your supporters.

Here are 3 ways to improve your LinkedIn profile so your donors feel good:

1. **Make sure it's 'public'.** Don't hide or your supporter will wonder why you won't let them learn more about you.

2. **Take a good picture.** Make sure you look happy. Smile! Your supporters won't want to meet a grouch!

3. **Improve your headline.** How about something like this?: "I help amazing people find meaning in their lives through support of _____."

WHEN IT COMES TO "MOVES MANAGEMENT," ARE YOU CONCERNED TOO?

First, what are we really talking about when we say *moves management*?

Wikipedia says, "moves are the actions an organization takes to bring in donors, establish relationships, and renew contributions."[7]

So, *moves* are what the fundraiser does. Ah! Moves are *activities*. I get it! Fundraisers achieve their goals if they develop plans for their activities. Moves management in fundraising is the development of plans and activities to raise money.

But then Wikipedia continues by saying, "David Dunlop, the Cornell University senior development officer who developed the concept of moves management, described the idea as "changing people's attitudes so they want to give."

Is that what moves management is really all about? Persuasion?

Hmmm.

Even David Dunlop once said, "People start 'making moves' and making a game of moves, rather than really recognizing the process that we're a part of is inspiring people to do the things that we believe they would want to do anyway. Really helping them accomplish what is consistent with their values and interests. It's a different perspective than fancy asking or skillful asking."[8]

Structure and process.

Ok. So I'm all in when it comes to making strategic plans for each donor. Doing so is smart because it keeps a fundraiser focused on who and what is important. It helps them think about the individual needs of each donor, how

---

7 https://en.wikipedia.org/wiki/Moves_management
8 https://leadershipphilanthropy.com/so-i-asked-dave-dunlop-is-moves-management-misunderstood/

CHAPTER THREE: GENERAL FUNDRAISING

they can add value for each donor and how they can make each donor feel good. This kind of thoughtful donor-centricity and careful planning helps fundraisers stay on task so they generate money to support the good work of their organizations and institutions.

The system works because it helps fundraisers remain patient, persistent and attentive to donor needs as they pursue worthy goals.

Plus, structure and process yields results. In the 2017 Major Gifts Benchmark Study[9] (an effort I funded), it was determined that fundraisers using a consistent process to identify prospects are more likely to achieve their fundraising goals. So structure and process are essential if you want results.

For-profits do it too!

For-profit businesses use something called TAPS (Target Account Planning Strategies). The idea is very similar to moves management and applies to large deals.

Sales people and/or their managers select target accounts. Then they do their homework to learn about the needs of all the influencers involved in the decision (since each of them might experience different pain points that need to be addressed and served). Next, they develop step-by-step plans for communications and engagements that help align the sales person's solutions with the needs of those people. Their plans include dates, responsibility assignments, and milestones.

With TAPS, a spirit of partnership is essential (just like in moves management).

So why am I concerned?

The first time I heard the phrase *moves management* I thought the process might involve trickery and manipulation. As a donor, I wondered, "Are they making moves on me? Are they trying to manage me?" No one really wants

---

[9] http://imarketsmart.com/2017benchmarkstudy/

to feel like they are being played, right?

Now before you start typing an angry response to this post telling me you are insulted because you are not a manipulative louse, remember, Wikipedia said David Dunlop described the idea as "changing people's attitudes." Let's face it, there's a very thin line between persuasion and manipulation.

Of course, you and I both know that there's no underhandedness going on here. But, for some, the inference remains and I have definitely met fundraisers who believe it is their job to *move* donors through the consideration process rather than to help the donors **move themselves** by providing engagement offers that deliver value.

Am I just splitting hairs?

Although the phrase 'moves management' is just an in-house term, I guess I just don't like it. Sure, thanks to alliteration, the phrase sounds great. It flows from your lips to your manager's and board member's ears so nicely. But I just can't get the thought of fundraisers manipulating donors out of my mind even though that's not what they're doing.

I know, I'm not a fundraiser. So maybe I'll never 'get' it. I'm just the CEO of a for-profit business (but I am a donor).

What do you think?

Are they really *moves*? Aren't they really actions, tasks or activities? Why confuse things and possibly lead some to wonder if they're being manipulated? Do you like the phrase? Do you use it?

CHAPTER THREE: GENERAL FUNDRAISING

IS SHAMING AN EFFECTIVE FUNDRAISING STRATEGY?

I was intrigued.

A few weeks ago one of my employees (Nicole) forwarded the following email to me from her beloved alma mater. It was from the president of the school. Impressive!

The subject line made clear that he was going to let her know how she can help the University of _____. "That's interesting," I thought to myself. I wondered if she felt that the University had helped her so much that she would want to return the favor. So I asked Nicole how she felt before I read any further. Her answer: "No."

Storm clouds were gathering.

Based on her answer I knew she didn't forward the email to me because it was inspirational. No, it was a doozy.

It began with some bragging about the fact that the Princeton Review said the University of _____ was named the Best ____ College in America. Should we assume that they won the award because he is so awesome?

Then, he quickly changed gears and began to grumble about how much he wished alumni (like Nicole) could see how amazing he is (Oops! I meant to say how amazing the school is). After all, the Princeton Review could see it.

Next, he lamented that Nicole clearly is not "in the know" and is apparently not proud of her school because she, and so many others like her, are not giving as much as their peers at other schools. The insult wasn't enough though. He continued by piling on some stats about her and her friends' failure to give. He hinted that the low participation rate is making him look bad in public. And finally, he wrapped it up with a weak attempt at highlighting some benefits she might gain from giving.

According to him, here are some of the benefits Nicole could enjoy if she'd just give:
- She could help him build momentum by giving early in the year
- She could readily and actively demonstrate her pride
- She could encourage greater percentages of alumni to give in the months to come

Those are some pretty weak benefits.

Followed by some stronger benefits... finally!
- She could help to support academic excellence
- She could help make the school affordable and accessible to future students (but not for her)
- She could help support financial aid (just not to help her pay-off her debts)

Although these are stronger benefits, they don't really satisfy Nicole's needs. Folks, people don't give when they finally understand your organization's needs. They give when your organization finally understands their needs!

So did she give?

No. Although she still has too much student debt and other priorities, the real reason she kept her money in her wallet was because the email he sent made her feel bad, not good. It's that simple.

I can't imagine that the approach was successful. What do you think? Would you give in response to this appeal?

———- Forwarded message ———-
From: President Xxxxx Xxxxxxxxxx
Date: Tue, Sep 12, 2017
Subject: How You Can Help
Dear Nicole:

In the past few months a variety of college rankings have focused on the University of _____. The Princeton Review named us the "Best

CHAPTER THREE: GENERAL FUNDRAISING

____ College in America" while the Fiske Guide to Colleges credited us for "first-of-their-kind academic programs and innovative out-of-classroom learning and networking opportunities," that drive _____'s "vision of preprofessional education shaped by commitments to the liberal arts, leadership, and community involvement." Fiske also recognized our deep commitment to preparing students for life and work, and the unique ways we go about it.

One of my most fervent hopes is that _____ alumni see _____ as clearly as others do, that they are proud of their association with the extraordinary school they attended, and that their knowledge and pride would be reflected in a commitment of support for their alma mater. So many of the things that make us proudest of this University were made possible by the involvement and generosity of alumni. But in order for the University to continue to flourish into the future, we need the help of all dedicated _____.

During the past five years, more than half of our undergraduate alumni have made a gift to the University. That's over 18,000 _____s, and I am deeply grateful to each and every one of you. Yet _____'s annual alumni participation rate is below the level of our peers, hovering under 25%, and does not accurately reflect the pride of our _____ community. Aside from the critical contribution that private philanthropy makes to our continued growth and progress, this matters because giving participation is the most publicly recognized measure of alumni loyalty and satisfaction. Based on my interaction with alumni over the past two years, I am convinced that less than 25% participation does not reflect the _____ pride of our alumni community.

How can you help? By making a gift each year to the annual fund or to the areas of school life that have meant the most to you. By making your gift now, early in the school year, you help us build momentum, readily and actively demonstrate your pride, and encourage greater percentages of alumni giving in the months to come.

SMARTIDEAS: THE BEST OF 2017

Your gift helps to support academic excellence and makes _____ affordable and accessible to future _____s. It also supports financial aid and the programs, experiences, and opportunities admired and heralded by Fiske and others. It is also an excellent investment, ensuring effective stewardship of your charitable giving, as The Princeton Review ranking attests.

Thank you for your help with this important effort that supports your University and our students. Together we can show the depth of _____ Pride and add the category of strong alumni participation to _____'s many publicly recognized accolades.

To make a gift right now, please go to givenow.-xxxxxxxx-.edu.
Best wishes, and go _____s!
Xxxxxxx Xxxxxxxxx
President

P.S. I hope to see you back on campus for Homecoming on October 26-28!

P.P.S. If this email has crossed paths with your gift, please accept my heartfelt gratitude.

CHAPTER THREE: GENERAL FUNDRAISING

YOU'VE GOT LEADS (IDENTIFIED MAJOR DONOR PROSPECTS) BUT ARE THEY 'OUTREACH-READY'?

People and vendors in our sector talk a lot about identifying donors, but getting them ready to meet with you is a different story.

The problem is that most donors simply aren't ready to talk to you yet.

This post was inspired by a horrible meeting.

Last week, I met with the Vice President of University Relations at one of the biggest schools in the country. During our chat, I told her that most 'identified' major and planned gift prospects need to be cultivated before outreach.

My statement was met with a grimace and the following response: "That's not what we train fundraisers to do. We train them to reach out to prospects as soon as they're identified."

"This meeting isn't gonna' go well," I thought to myself silently.

Then she said, "You know… I've been doing this for 30 years."

"Hmm. Just because you've been doing things for decades doesn't mean you're doing them correctly," I mused (again silently).

I wondered if she had ever donated because, in my experience, as a donor, when fundraisers move too fast they make supporters very uncomfortable. No one likes receiving cold calls (and no one enjoys making them).

You can avoid discomfort on both sides if you segment your data as follows:
- **Identified supporters** – These folks have been found to meet certain requirements according to basic engagement and giving metrics (or wealth screening and predictive modeling)

- **Qualified supporters** – If you don't have budget for wealth screening or other forms of prospect identification, you can easily skip that expense and qualify your major and planned giving prospects/donors using a donor survey (of course, I built the only donor survey platform that really gets the job done for people like you). Using that tool you'll capture each donor's interests, passions and a lot more. Then you can use that information in the next stage below.

- **Qualified supporters in cultivation** – Once you have qualified your leads and collected great information about them, their interests and their desires, next you'll need to prioritize them for outreach (unless you have the staff and free time to call all of your qualified leads). But even if you have that kind of free time, we have found that interrupting them with cold calls (as the Vice President in my story demands of her 'well-trained' staff) is challenging. Gaining a warm referral from a solid mutual connection works better. But if you don't have one of those, you might want to let most of them self-navigate the stages of the relationship by leveraging technology to deliver highly relevant, personalized email 'touches' that never ask for money but, instead, provide value and deliver meaningful content. This builds trust. Technology also helps you manage the very tedious and time-consuming cultivation and prioritization process. It's not easy for a Gift Officer to do it right. Staying on top of cultivation efforts for dozens, hundreds or thousands of qualified major gift or legacy supporters is just too complex. Artificial intelligence can do it for you at very low cost.

- **Highly qualified 'outreach-ready' supporters** – As their trust and desire grow over time thanks to your hi-value, highly-personalized, meaningful and highly relevant cultivation, they'll eventually be ready for you to reach out to them. Also, at this stage they'll be exponentially more likely to accept your outreach, meet with you and give. Your call won't be cold. It will be warm or even hot. Some supporters will even thank you for your attentiveness and concern. (NOTE: You'll know when that time arrives if you monitor their digital body language using our platform.)

CHAPTER THREE: GENERAL FUNDRAISING

Voila! Highly-qualified outreach-ready leads.

In the private sector they are called 'sales-ready leads'. Of course, fundraisers are not salespeople. So for our sector I like to call them 'outreach-ready leads'. These are highly qualified leads that have been nurtured and cultivated properly over time so, when you reach out to them, they don't feel like they're being attacked. Rather, they're 'ready' to accept your outreach. In most cases they even welcome it and thank you for finally contacting them.

If you don't have highly qualified outreach-ready major and legacy giving leads, maybe it's time for you to talk to us. It's easy to do so. Visit imarketsmart.com to learn more.

DONOR PSYCHOLOGY: DO YOU KNOW WHAT REALLY MAKES YOUR SUPPORTERS FEEL GOOD?

Funny thing about fundraising is that it all boils down to this: Making sure that your supporters feel good!

I know, I know. In the books and webinars, they'll say, "It's all about proving impact and results." Others will say, "It's all about relationships." And, yet, many more will say, "It's all about the mission." But I'm here to say that it's really all about simply making sure your supporters feel good. And, they will if you give them great experiences, add value to their lives, and provide extraordinary customer service!

So now the question is: Do you know what will make each major donor and each planned gift lead or supporter feel good about their decision give to your organization?

I'll give you a hint, it probably has very little to do with charts and statistics about impact and more to do with something personal. Proving impact only assures donors that you're doing good with their money. It reduces donor remorse and builds trust.

Some people might be lonely. Getting involved might quench their thirst for a connection. Give them that opportunity and they'll feel good.

Others might want to memorialize someone they love. Give them a chance to do that and you'll make them feel good.

Many simply want a shot of dopamine to lift their spirits up. Enable their giving and you'll make them feel good.

Get the idea?

Bottom line: Find out what really makes each of your donors feel good and you'll raise more money.
These days, finding that out is easier than ever. There's a donor survey

CHAPTER THREE: GENERAL FUNDRAISING

platform that raises money and generates leads. How do I know?.... I invented it!

After generating millions of responses from donors in 4 countries around the world, we've read a lot of reasons why people give. Below are most of the reasons they relayed through our platform to benefit our clients' fundraising efforts.

Giving produces a warm glow
Giving lifts them up and makes them feel alive
Giving sets their heart on fire
Giving ignites their emotions
Giving provides them with spiritual sensation
Giving supports the practice of their religion
Giving provides them with a sense of community
Giving brings them closer to others
Giving makes them famous (sometimes)
Giving provides them with notoriety
Giving allows them to right wrongs
Giving enables them to "give back"
Giving brings them perks or tax benefits
Giving allays their guilt or heals their pain
Giving makes them feel like a hero in their own life story
Giving supports their pursuit of meaning in their lives
Giving enables them to honor or memorialize someone
Giving allows them to feel like they will leave a legacy
Giving makes them feel good

THE SIMPLEST AND MOST EFFECTIVE 6-STEP MAJOR GIFT AND PLANNED GIFT MARKETING STRATEGY EVER

1. Employ donor surveys.
2. Provide valuable engagement offers using the information you learned from the surveys (that way your offers will elicit responses— since you now know what your prospects want/desire).
3. Use technology that tracks and captures their online engagements (clicks, downloads, etc.).
4. Use technology that "drips" highly relevant, personalized cultivation communications to each prospect based on how they have interacted online and offline in the past. Also, pay attention to what they have said when responding to the donor surveys.
5. And, most important, use technology that scores each prospects engagement, passion, and likelihood to make a major gift based on 20 years of research data.

If your marketing strategy doesn't include these steps, you are probably costing your organization a lot of money. Don't you owe it to your supporters to steward their funds by cutting costs while raising more money more efficiently?

REQUEST A DEMO WITH US AND WE'LL SHOW YOU HOW PEOPLE JUST LIKE YOU ARE SUCCEEDING WITH THIS 6-STEP STRATEGY. www.imarketsmart.com

CHAPTER THREE: GENERAL FUNDRAISING

WHY MISTAKES ARE AWESOME AND WHAT TO DO ABOUT THEM

I know the feeling. A supporter calls to tell you your email or letter spelled her name wrong. She's pissed! You begin to sweat and your muscles become tense. You think to yourself – "This sucks!"

But what you really should be thinking is, "This is a terrific opportunity to make things right and build a deeper relationship with a supporter who cared enough to call." Let's face it, if the supporter wanted the relationship to be over, they never would have called you in the first place.

They don't want it to end. They just want to be heard. They want you to make things right.

Yes! These events ARE opportunities disguised as complaints.

Amazon.com's mission statement is: "To be Earth's most customer-centric company where people can find and discover anything they want to buy online." Jeff Bezos once said, "We see our customers as invited guests to a party, and we are the hosts. It's our job every day to make every important aspect of the customer experience a little bit better."

Wow! They want to be the most customer-centric company on the entire planet and they do it by behaving like hosts!

And what about Disney? Walt Disney himself once said, "Give the public everything you can give them."

Finally, Donald Porter of British Airways said, "Customers don't expect you to be perfect. They DO expect you to fix things when they go wrong."

The MarketSmart takeaway here is that your supporters will continue to support your mission and will actually dig deeper to give more if you:

SMARTIDEAS: THE BEST OF 2017

First, be glad they called.
Second, respond promptly.
Third, apologize profusely— and mean it! Be real!
Fourth, bend over backwards to make it right.
Fifth, make sure you made it right.
Sixth, thank them for allowing you the opportunity to make it right.

CHAPTER THREE: GENERAL FUNDRAISING

TOP 10 WAYS YOU CAN BENEFIT FROM CONDUCTING A DONOR SURVEY

1. **Raise money** – If you want advice, ask for money. If you want money ask for advice. Surveys raise money.

2. **Identify** – Decide who your best donor prospects are based on what they say.

3. **Generate leads** – Get major donor and legacy gift prospects to raise their hands showing interest in giving or volunteering.

4. **Qualify** – Ensure that you spend your time wisely with hi-capacity, passionate, motivated supporters.

5. **Prioritize** – Determine who requires attention most urgently.

6. **Capture vital information** – Uncover demographic information you simply can't buy while learning why each supporter cares, their life story, and their wants, needs, interests and desires so you can cultivate the relationship properly and have meaningful one-to-one conversations.

7. **Understand** – Where each donor prospect resides in the consideration process for giving so you focus on those who are ready.

8. **Gain referrals** – Inspire hi-value, major gift supporters to refer you to like-minded friends and family members.

9. **Clean up your list** – When done right, 7% of survey respondents will update their contact information for you.

10. **Deliver value** – Surveying your supporters makes them feel valued and appreciated.

CHAPTER FOUR:
Engagement Fundraising

SMARTIDEAS: THE BEST OF 2017

CHAPTER FOUR: ENGAGEMENT FUNDRAISING

8 SIMPLE IDEAS TO INVOLVE YOUR DONORS AND BUILD DEEPER CONNECTIONS

L.M. Montgomery was a famous author in the early 1900's. Her novels were internationally renowned. She once said, "Tell me and I forget. Teach me and I remember. Involve me and I learn."

This is so true. Involvement is one of the best ways to build seriously deep connections. It can mean the difference between no gift and the ultimate gift. There are millions of ways you can do this. Here are eight of them:
1. Be transparent and give them access with a personal tour
2. Help them meet your staff, your volunteers, and the folks that benefit from their donations
3. Write them a personal letter
4. Ask a beneficiary to write them a letter (such as a child that received a healthy meal from your homeless shelter)
5. Reach out personally on social media
6. Conduct a Webinar
7. Send them pictures or videos showing them the results of their support
8. Invite them to volunteer

….the list goes on and on. How are you involving your most valuable donors?

SMARTIDEAS: THE BEST OF 2017

THE 8 CORE COMPONENTS OF ENGAGEMENT FUNDRAISING AND WHY YOU DESPERATELY NEED THEM

Most fundraising is based on what I call "single shot" strategies.

For instance, it's an event, gala or golf outing. Or, perhaps it's a mailing, an email blast or a social media campaign. And, it could even be a face-to-face visit, a tour of your facilities, or a webinar.

Sure, you might use multiple channels to promote what you're doing. In that case, you'll label your effort "multi-channel" or "integrated."

But, no matter what you're doing or what you call it, usually it will achieve short-term results targeting one particular kind of gift (usually cash but sometimes a planned gift). A single shot!

CHAPTER FOUR: ENGAGEMENT FUNDRAISING

It's expensive and time-consuming. It's inefficient because it fails to optimize your staff and resources. But that's how short-term gain works and as many fundraisers say, "that's the way we've always done it."

But that's not the way it has to be.

A better way (by leaps and bounds) is what I call Engagement Fundraising — the term I coined in 2012. Here are the 8 components of my innovative fundraising methodology.

1. Acceptance of the Pareto Principle.

This is also known as the 80/20 Rule. But when it comes to fundraising it's more like the 90/10 Rule. Basically, the concept recognizes that 90% of your dollars will come from just 10% of your donors. Plus, it applies to planned gifts, too. Ninety percent of your planned gift dollars will come from just 10% of your planned gift donors.

2. Understanding of why people really give.

People give because it makes them feel good. It's simple. But knowing that doesn't make it easier to raise money. Knowing that just puts you on the right footing. It steers you towards an attitude of customer service, empathy, facilitation, and concern. Knowing this ensures that your fundraising efforts – now aimed at those with tremendous capacity thanks to the acceptance of the Pareto Principle – will become customer service oriented. Knowing this ensures that people become partners, not targets. They become human beings with feelings, stories and passions, not ATM machines with buttons you press to get the money your boss wants you from them.

3. Employment of a feedback loop.

Most nonprofits don't listen very much to their supporters because it's challenging to listen to so many voices. So, unfortunately, instead, they just spray messages at them. It's mostly one-way. Yours! But listening is an essential part of any dialogue. You simply can't build trusting, committed relationships without genuine dialogue. And, you can't raise money without trusting, committed relationships. Therefore, listening must become at least 80% of your communication strategy.

But how can you listen to hundreds, thousands or millions of supporter voices? It's only possible if you employ technologies to capture your supporters' "verbatims" (self-reported information) and digital body language (online engagement including clicks, views, downloads, time online, recency of their online visit, how frequently they engage online, how much time they spend on your site, and so on). Of course, right now MarketSmart is the only technology firm that offers these kinds of technologies to support the fundraising sector. They help fundraisers cut costs, optimize what they do, and raise big gifts efficiently. The feedback loop is deployed in our donor survey, micro-site and automated "drip" email platforms.

But, you can cobble together your own feedback loop using your own tools for donor surveys, online chat tools, micro-sites, telemarketing efforts, face-to-face encounters and so on. It's expensive but it can be done.

4. Valuable engagement offers.

Once you accept the Pareto Principle, understand why people give and begin to employ a feedback loop, you'll need to draw people into your marketing funnel. This is where it gets fun and interesting because the development of valuable engagement offers frees you from interruptive, off-putting, spray-and-pray fundraising outreach efforts. Instead, offers give you a chance to give to your donors (rather than asking them to give to you).

The law of reciprocity states that you are more likely to receive if you give first. Plus, it has been proven that the person who gives first usually receives a gift in return from the original recipient that far exceeds the value of the first person's gift (by exponential measures).

Providing valuable engagement offers proves to your supporters that you care about them. In fact, you can tie the first three components (mentioned above) together with this one to provide your hi-capacity supporters an opportunity to fill out a donor survey so they can express why they care, how they want to give and when. Doing so will make them feel good. I know

CHAPTER FOUR: ENGAGEMENT FUNDRAISING

because MarketSmart has sent out millions of donor surveys on behalf of our clients each year and their supporters show their appreciation by giving more. A lot more!

Interestingly, we even ask our clients' supporters (for instance) if they have Donor Advised Funds and if they'd consider making ("recommending") a donation with their own. Then, on the Thank You Page after the survey, only the respondents who said "Yes" to that question get an opportunity to do just that. And they do (at an average donation of over $4,000)!

There are other kinds of engagement offers that will draw your supporters closer to your mission. For some charities, the best ones might be webinars, free content, checklists, and so on. At MarketSmart we have "productized" dozens of offers we know work. But if you don't want us to help, you can develop your own offers using this checklist for free.

Bottom line: Your offers shouldn't always involve an 'ask' for your supporters and prospects to give you money. That drives them crazy. Instead, your offers should engage your major and planned gift prospects and supporters in ways that make them feel good. Then, thanks to the law of reciprocity, they'll return the favor by exponential measures.

5. Lead generation efforts.

Once you have developed your offers aimed at hi-capacity donors and buttressed by a feedback loop that makes them feel good, you'll want to generate leads. In other words, you'll want to present the offers to your list in a way that helps you qualify people who are likely to make major and/or planned gifts.

At this stage, it is important to recognize that the most important part of any lead generation effort is your approach. Your outreach must be polite and considerate. You must always ask for permission to communicate with your constituents. Ask them to opt-in and make it easy for them to opt-out. Make sure your efforts are highly contextual, highly personalized and highly relevant.

Stop spraying and praying. It's disrespectful and mean. Gaining permission is fair, it invites collaboration and it builds trust. You should only want people in your funnel because they want to be there. Forcing them to be there will never result in more donations. You can't wash money out of your supporters' bank accounts with a hose! Stop spraying and praying!

Present your valuable engagement offers to the right people at the right times. Let them lean in. Make it easy for them to accept your offers. Then capture the information they provide about their interests, wants, needs and desires using landing pages (online forms) and tracking tools that gather their "verbatims" and digital body language.

6. Cultivation efforts.

Generating leads is almost a complete waste if you don't have a plan to cultivate them. Cultivation allures people (now your qualified leads) to engage further. Cultivation gives you a chance to show them that you know them, that you listened, that you care about their needs, and that they are important to you. Everyone on earth wants to feel important and feel good. Deliberate, meaningful cultivation "drips" are where the magic really happens as long as they are persistent yet polite, personalized and relevant.

The problem for most fundraisers is that cultivation is tedious and time-consuming. You and your staff are already overworked, your data warehouses are a mess and your staff keeps leaving or changing positions. You know this step is essential but how on earth can you get it right? Mechanized automation is the most effective and efficient way to provide proper cultivation that builds trust and earns respect. And, thanks to our technology (the Giftmaker+ system), now you can "drip" the right emails to the right people at the right times. If you're not employing these technologies (especially with email drips), you're missing the "yeast that will make the bread rise."

7. Dashboard.

By now you're probably starting to wonder how on earth you'd be able to capture all of the data and prioritize who you should call (and when). I bet

CHAPTER FOUR: ENGAGEMENT FUNDRAISING

you already know where I'm going with this. You'll need a dashboard that helps you see your funnel so you can take action. A well-designed dashboard is the glue that ties it all together. It provides clarity, it serves up leads and it helps you see who is ready for personal outreach. Want to see ours? Just reach out to us. We'll show it to you. Hundreds of fundraisers just like you around the world use it and love it!

8. Conversion efforts.

Finally, you'll need to ask for the gift at some point, right? The idea that supports Engagement Fundraising is that most of your supporters care and want to give. It's just that they usually aren't ready to give when you want them to do so. That's because most of the time you're guessing when you should spray your 'asks' at them.

With these eight core components in place, you'll finally be able to know when to ask. Marrying that crucial piece of information with your supporters' sense of trust and desire for reciprocation (that each donor will have if they are cultivated properly) makes serious magic happen. Then you need to be there to facilitate their giving (by answering their questions and closing the gift). The world needs fundraisers like you to facilitate their giving. Your efforts seal the deal. Strategic, innovative technologies can't work without you.

If your fundraising efforts don't include these 8 components, you are behind the curve.

MarketSmart now has hundreds of clients in 4 countries around the world using our Engagement Fundraising model along with our proprietary scoring algorithm and dashboard. They are building better relationships with their donors (who by the way might have previously been your donors). Our clients' gifts are getting bigger. They are retaining donors at astounding rates. All while your donors are either reducing the amounts they give to your organization or ending their giving to your organization entirely because you failed to treat them the way our clients treat them.

Are you ready to win them back? If so, let us know. We'll help you.

3 NEW PHRASES/CONCEPTS ENGAGEMENT FUNDRAISERS NEED TO KNOW

If you've been reading this blog for a while, you know that I coined the phrase "engagement fundraising" in 2013. But if you haven't done a demo with us recently you probably haven't heard these new phrases/concepts. That's why I'm sharing them with you today.

These phrases/concepts are important to know and understand if you want to succeed in today's demanding fundraising environment.

1. Feedback loops – Communication channels that provide real-time information reporting so you can make adjustments to optimize the timing and content of your messages to your prospects and supporters. Nonprofits habitually employ absent feedback loops for outbound direct mail, email (spam, not permission email), and telemarketing to achieve their fundraising objectives without listening carefully to their constituents' reactions and responses. Everything works much better and raises more money when communications have been developed to satisfy each receiver's interests, needs, wants, hopes and desires.

2. Verbatims – These are the exact words your prospects and supporters have used to tell you their interests, needs, wants, hopes and desires. You can capture them if you have developed, employed, and optimized your feedback loops. The best way to capture verbatims is through the use of donor surveys.

3. Digital body language – Everyone knows about body language—nonverbal communication such as facial expressions, body posture, gestures, eye movements, etc. But digital body language is different. It includes the nonverbal actions online such as clicks, forwards, likes, downloads, views, visits, time-on-site, etc.

Digital body language and verbatims are two sides of the same coin. Both should be part of your feedback loop so you can treat your constituents better and raise exponentially more dollars at much lower costs.

CHAPTER FOUR: ENGAGEMENT FUNDRAISING

If you aren't using them and don't have the technology or dashboard needed to harness their power, you really should get a demo and see how you can.

THE 5 P'S OF ENGAGEMENT FUNDRAISING

1- Permission

Donors have immense power these days. They can ignore your communications! The best way to ensure that they don't exercise that power is to gain their permission to communicate with them. Having a list of 100,000 matters little if no one engages with your outreach.

You can gain permission if you develop content (engagement experiences, tools, widgets, videos, workbooks, apps, etc.) that provides value to your target audience of potential donors. As they benefit from what you're providing, ask them to consider opting-in to have a relationship.

Then ask them to tell you about their interests and passions so you can do your best to communicate with them relevantly. The best way to do that is with a survey.

2- Personalization

If you think personalization is about putting a person's name on a letter or email, think again. It's about a lot more than that.

Once you've gained permission, you must prove over and over that you won't abuse the privilege you just attained by over-communicating irrelevantly. Show them that you care by demonstrating that you listened. Personalize your communications with relevant content and offers that reflect each individual's interests and passions.

3- Participation

Involvement leads to commitment. Get people to participate!

Any level of association will do. Offer opportunities for arms-length participation such as a chance to view a webinar, hear a podcast or use an app. Or offer chances for deeper engagement such as board leadership, committee involvement, etc.

CHAPTER FOUR: ENGAGEMENT FUNDRAISING

Wondering which participation offer to send to an individual? The offer should match their interests and consideration stage.

4- Persistence

Most fundraising is very short-sighted. Yet, the turtle beats the hare every time. If you are focused on the Pareto Principle (which you should be), remain slow and steady. Don't give up and your persistence will pay off.

But remember to be novel. Persistence isn't about redundancy. Don't send the same thing to the same person over and over. Being creative and original will attract attention and interest.

5- Patience

Patience proves your commitment to success. It also proves that you care about your relationship with your supporters. You won't push them too far, too fast just to get another donation. You won't abuse the permission they granted.

It shows to your donors that you realize that great things take time and that their timetables matter more than yours because you care about them. Being patient confirms to them that you just want to make them feel good and you're in it for the long haul— just like they want to be.

ENGAGEMENT FUNDRAISING IN 7 SIMPLE BULLET-POINTS

- **Focus** - Focus your marketing (especially your expensive marketing like face-to-face meetings) on people who have a lot of money

- **Generate leads** - Generate highly-qualified leads among people who have a lot of money using a survey

- **Prioritize** - Prioritize the leads (hot, warm, cool, cold, and opt-out)

- **Arrange calls and visits** - Reach out to meet with the hot (and some warm) leads

- **Cultivate** - Cultivate the rest of the leads over time with highly personalized, relevant engagement offers that reflect their interests and make them feel good (based on what they said in the survey)

- **Mix up the soup bowl** - Continue engaging politely, consistently, and persistently while always offering your leads opportunities to move forward in the consideration process or opt-out

- **Build relationships with hi-value supporters at low cost** - Leverage technology as an inexpensive way to build the relationship

CHAPTER FOUR: ENGAGEMENT FUNDRAISING

WHAT FUNDRAISERS CAN LEARN FROM RESTAURANTS AND WAITERS

People give billions of dollars each year to waiters for a lot of the same reasons they give to charities.

1. Social conformity (simply because it's something you are supposed to do)
2. Reciprocity (in exchange for something of value – service)
3. Appreciation (recognition that the service was good)
4. Sympathy
5. Empathy
Etc.

But what else can we learn from the tips we *give* (unrestricted spending that is certainly not required) to restaurant waiters?

Frequency

"Customers who visited the restaurant 5 or more times per year left a larger tip (after controlling bill size) than did customers who visited the restaurant fewer than 5 times per year."

And…

Service

"People also tipped more, the more favorably they evaluated their service."

So what's the takeaway that fundraisers can learn from restaurants?

I think this reinforces my philosophy that quality engagement is the key to more revenue.

Of course, we all know that visiting with donors results in more and larger donations. So this philosophy probably comes as no surprise to you. But I think that quality engagement can be scaled-up thanks to technology these days. Now you can reach more supporters with high-quality "touches" more *frequently*, thereby providing better *service* and more value for your supporters and tremendously decreasing costs for your organization.

Now you can do more with less. You can engage more frequently and provide better service. And, if you do, I'll bet you'll increase your tips!

CHAPTER FOUR: ENGAGEMENT FUNDRAISING

CHAPTER FIVE:
Planned Giving

CHAPTER FIVE: PLANNED GIVING

NEWS FLASH: MOST OF YOUR SUPPORTERS DON'T REALLY WANT TO BE IN YOUR LEGACY SOCIETY

But, oddly, that's the first thing fundraisers offer legacy gift prospects and those who have disclosed their legacy gift intentions.

The next most popular offer is a pin.

I think these offers are pretty lame. Most of your supporters don't really want to be in your legacy society. And they didn't leave your organization in their will to get a pin.

So what do they want? Here's a good list for starters:

- A sense of community
- A feeling of involvement
- A way to see first-hand how their money will be used
- A way to be honored and appreciated so they can feel like a hero in their own life story
- A way to commemorate or memorialize someone who inspired them
- An opportunity to share why they care and tell their story
- A "thank you" every once in a while
- An invitation to have lunch perhaps

Can you think of some other reasons why they'd want to be in your Legacy Society?

If so, use those reasons to create offers that provide your supporters with value and make them feel good. Then they will want to be in your Legacy Society after all.

COUNT LEGACY GIFT DOLLARS, NOT PROMISES

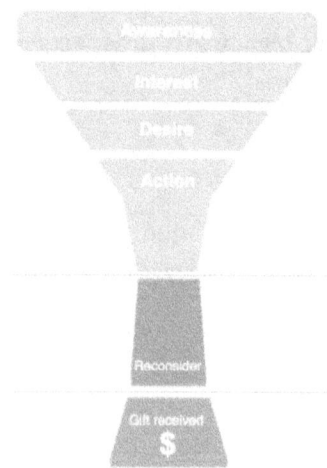

Total potential universe that could consider a legacy gift: Members, donors, advocates, volunteers, etc.

Interest: How many of those people have shown interest or have said they would consider a legacy gift?

Desire: How many are considering a legacy gift right now (engaging with you)?

Action: How many have taken action? Out of those, how many are irrevocable?

Consideration continuum: How many are being stewarded and where are each of them when it comes to keeping their commitment?

The goal for legacy gift fundraising is to raise money right?

In sports they say it doesn't matter how many points you score, it's whether you win the game. Counting Legacy Society members is counting points. It's good, but it should not be your primary focus.

Yet, unfortunately, way too many nonprofits (leaders and staff) focus mostly on getting supporters to say that the organization is in their plan (thereby increasing the size of the Legacy Society).

I'm sure there are lots of reasons for this focus. For instance:

1. It's a metric that is easy to count

2. It's a metric that is easy to get supporters to commit to (it's easier to get them to say the organization is in their plan than to ensure that the gift *remains* in their plan)

3. It's a metric that is easy for a short-timer (someone who job-hops) to focus on

CHAPTER FIVE: PLANNED GIVING

The problem with this focus

It encourages getting people to say, "You're in my plan" rather than "How can I give more?", "How can I get more involved?", or/and "How can we build an even deeper, more meaningful and mutually beneficial relationship over time?"

Realized dollars

If in addition to counting commitments, we focus heavily on realized dollars, then the planned giving fundraising strategy will be aligned properly with the desired result.

But there's one big problem with that too

You probably already thought to yourself, "But realized dollars require people to die… and that won't happen for a long time." So, how can we focus on realized dollars without sitting around waiting for people to die?

Focus instead on the funnel

Let's face it. People can ultimately change their minds. And you can be sure they won't tell you about their change of heart. So, ultimately, it does you and your organization no good to populate your Legacy Society with names if they don't turn into realized dollars.

The private sector focuses on funnels to build pipelines of predictable revenue. I think the nonprofit sector should, too. By doing so, the metrics will help you and your Board understand what's really going on.

Here are some metrics I suggest you consider as you build out your funnel:

Of course, you can add more to this funnel

This is a rough outline. But the basic idea is that you need to focus on the entire funnel, not just on counting promises. Once you do, you'll be able to assign dollar values to the numbers based on the realized dollars that actually come through over time.

It will take some time, effort and refinement. But once the funnel is developed, you'll have a much more reliable and honest way to measure what you are doing so you can see if it's working.

CHAPTER FIVE: PLANNED GIVING

HERE'S WHY WHEN IT COMES TO PLANNED GIFTS, IT ISN'T NECESSARILY ALL ABOUT THE RELATIONSHIPS

I have two questions that I ask people when they say that planned gift fundraising "is all about the relationship."

I ask, "How many gifts did you/your organization receive last year that 'came over the transom'? I also ask, "How many were not previously disclosed to you before you got the money or the call from the attorney?"

The answer is always something like, "70%, 80% or 90%."

After that, my reply usually packs a bit of a punch.

I ask, "So if it's 'all about the relationship,' how come you and your organization didn't know about so many gifts?"

I'm not trying to hurt anyone's feelings. It's just that I don't believe you can say that planned gift fundraising is 'all about the relationship' while, at the same time, have no idea about the vast proportion of gifts that have been planned for your nonprofit. Those two things don't add up.

So what's the point of this post?
1. I think we need to stop kidding ourselves and giving ourselves too much credit.
2. Yet, I think we need to recognize that a solid relationship with a supporter, advocate or member will definitely affect their legacy planning decisions. In that regard, solid, personal, 1-to-1 relationships are essential.
3. But, finally, we need to embrace the fact that the relationship is usually first and foremost with *the organization and its mission* (at least 70%, 80% or 90% of the time), not necessarily the fundraiser. By doing so, and by using technologies and strategies that enhance that relationship, you'll generate more planned gifts to support your cause.

SMARTIDEAS: THE BEST OF 2017

HOW TO STRUCTURE AND STAFF YOUR PLANNED GIFT SHOP FOR THE 21ST CENTURY

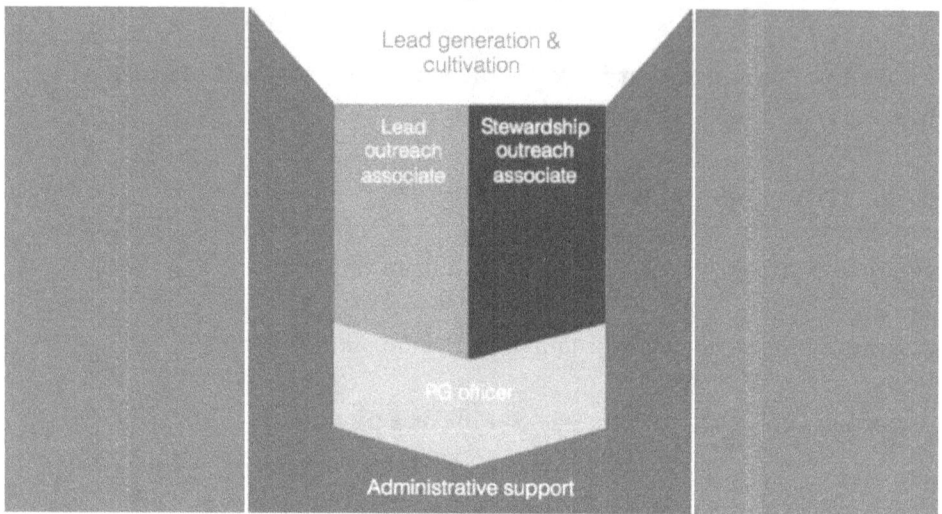

Jim Collins, author of the best-selling book Good to Great, has three big recommendations for all organizations:

- Get the right people on the bus
- *Get the right people in the right seats*
- Get the wrong people off the bus

So what does this mean for you?

I think nonprofits tend to fail when it comes to "getting the right people in the right seats." Too often they make people do things they don't want to do and/or aren't good at doing.

For instance, most Planned Gift Officers are great at helping donors employ myriad techniques to enhance their giving so everyone wins. Many are attorneys or estate planning experts who don't enjoy cold or warm calling to set meetings with donors. Yet most nonprofits force them to perform those tasks.

CHAPTER FIVE: PLANNED GIVING

I recommend aligning your staff properly with the following structure for the shop of the 21st century.

In the late 90's, the private sector (thanks to a guy named Aaron Ross) figured out that sales teams (like fundraising teams) were set up wrong. He was responsible for the massive growth Salesforce.com had back then thanks to his staff realignment ideas. But below you will find how I've adapted them for the nonprofit sector.

The basic concept relies on having "the right people on your bus." Then you need to optimize each person's performance by organizing what they do according to their unique skills, interests and talents. Doing so will yield focus and specialization that deliver much better results.

This is something I've been telling a lot of people all around the country and world. Some very smart people (like Richard Perry at Veritus Group) are buying-in to the concept and recommending it to their clients.

The structure of the properly aligned team looks like this:

Lead Outreach Associates – These people should only concentrate on setting up calls and or meetings so the PG Officer (technician) can spend most or all of their time helping donors, prospective PG donors, volunteers, staff, and others. Let's face it, many PG Officers that dislike outbound calling and emailing shouldn't be doing those tasks. Instead, why not break that part of their job off to let passionate, tenacious Lead Outreach Associates call the leads (and even make cold-calls to people too!). Lead Outreach Associates should become experts at engaging with donors relevantly and contextually at the right times.

Skills – Amiable and friendly people-person who is happy to do what skilled PG officers might be less interested in doing such as:
- Call, email, and connect on social media, etc.
- Provide value
- Build rapport and trust
- Collect information
- Further qualify the leads
- Set meetings and appointments with the Planned Gift Officer

Stewardship Associates – The biggest planned gift gains can happen fastest if Stewardship Associates provide Legacy Society members (and major donors) with first-class, red velvet rope, priority service ... stewardship! This is especially important for the wealthiest people in the group because, when it comes to planned gifts, at least 80% of the dollars of any PG program will usually come from less than 20% of the PG donors. Therefore, Stewardship Associates should work a strategic "customer service" plan aligning their limited efforts with the best opportunities. Remember, these gifts have not been realized yet and donors can change their minds at any time. Strategically placing service-minded staff here will ensure that gifts that have been disclosed and/or closed already will not be removed. Also, Stewardship Associates should always be on the lookout for new opportunities since the best place to get more planned gifts is from current Legacy Society Members. Like the Lead Outreach Associates, they should become experts at engaging with donors contextually, relevantly and at the right times.

Skills – Also amiable and friendly.
- Enhance the Legacy Society experience for the donors
- Generates leads for "upsells" (second and third legacy gift opportunities)
- Ensure that planned gifts become realized gifts
- Call, email, and connect on social media, etc.
- Provide value
- Build rapport and trust
- Collect information
- Attend to needs
- Deliver service
- Set meetings and appointments with the Planned Gift Officer

Planned Gift Officers/Technicians – The Lead Outreach Associates and Stewardship Associates are there to serve the donors and "tee-up" opportunities for the technical experts— the Planned Gift Officers. These people are usually amazing at taking opportunities (appointments set up by the Lead Outreach Associates and Stewardship Associates) and turning them into big bucks. Therefore, it's essential that they do what they are good at doing and they are not forced to do what the Lead Outreach Associates and Stewardship Associates can do much better. They should be booked! Their

CHAPTER FIVE: PLANNED GIVING

calendars should be filled (by the efforts of the Lead Outreach Associates and Stewardship Associates) with calls and face-to-face meetings every day from morning to night.

Skills – Exceptionally skilled at helping donors make gifts (especially big gifts)
- Work with each donor or their attorney or estate planner
- Handle technical details

<u>Bottom line</u>: Nonprofits should never try to combine and mash-up these roles. Doing so gets people doing too many things they're not good at doing. Putting people into "specializations" is the key to exponential gains and tremendous effectiveness. It's been proven effective in the private sector and I'm convinced it will work in the nonprofit sector, too.

What do you think? Do you agree with my concept? Think it will work?

CHAPTER SIX:
Major Gifts

SMARTIDEAS: THE BEST OF 2017

6 MAJOR DONOR EXPECTATIONS YOU SIMPLY CANNOT IGNORE

1. **Dialogue.** Major donors expect to be able to have a dialogue with an organization and its staff.
2. **Permission.** Major donors expect to maintain power over whether or not they grant permission for dialogue to happen.
3. **Convenience.** Major donors expect their engagements to be convenient for them.
4. **Focus.** Major donors expect you to focus on them (be relevant and provide value that suits their needs and desires).
5. **Self-directed.** Major donors expect to be able to self-direct their decision-making journey.
6. **Anonymous.** Major donors expect to have the opportunity to remain anonymous.

SMARTIDEAS: THE BEST OF 2017

HOW BIG IS THE AVERAGE MAJOR GIFT?

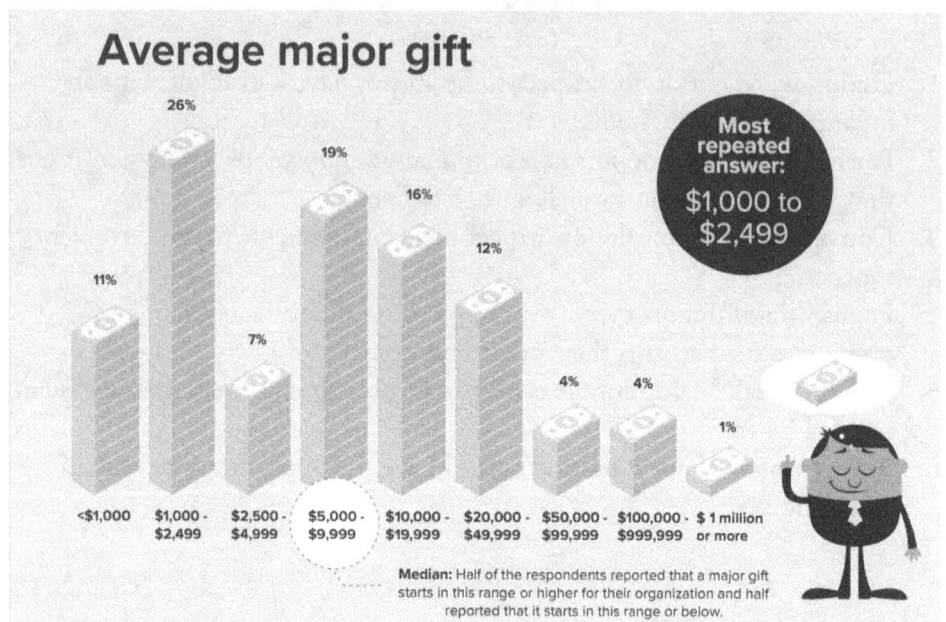

"What's your average?"

I found myself asking that question in meetings with clients all the time. What surprised me was that most didn't know the answer.

Most businesses know their numbers. Nonprofits usually know their overall *average donation* size. They might also know their *retention rate* too.

But when it comes to major gifts things get tricky because before the average amount can be determined, the organization has to first determine what qualifies as a major gift.

I decided to find the answer.

This was just one of the questions that led me to fund the first-ever study of its kind: The 2017 Major Gift Benchmark Study. You can download the infographic and report at imarketsmart.com/2017benchmarkstudy/ for free.

CHAPTER SIX: MAJOR GIFTS

To make it easier on fundraisers, we provided ranges from which they could select their average. What we found was this: The most-repeated answer: $1,000 – $2,499 (that's a pretty low dollar amount for an average **major** gift in my opinion).

The data gets broken down by sector, too. But you'll have to download the report to see how that breaks out.

Check it out and let me know what you think. And, please consider sharing the link with your colleagues so they can benefit from the information, too.

WHY YOUR WEALTHY DONORS LOVE DONOR ADVISED FUNDS AND WHY YOU SHOULD CARE

Donor Advised Funds… There are plenty of people who don't like 'em.

They say that they are holding pens for dollars that should be distributed to good causes faster. But that's not a debate I want to have here.

Instead, I want to point out why they work, why your donors love them and why you should care— NOW!

First, when marketing anything, it's essential to have a good product. One that makes people's lives better. Makes things easier, faster, etc.

Donor Advised Fund products are solid because they:
1. Provide donors with anonymity and privacy especially if they simply don't want to meet with a fundraiser.
2. Give them a tremendous sense of control and flexibility.
3. Deliver a really nice tax deduction.
4. Allow donors to make their giving decisions more carefully and at a time that is convenient for them on their timetable (not the charity's).
5. Are trustworthy.

You simply can't argue with this value proposition. It's pretty darn good.

CHAPTER SIX: MAJOR GIFTS

3 AMAZING QUOTES FROM MAJOR DONORS

Here are 3 amazing quotes from major donors worth reading:

"I walk over to my desk, take out my pen, and get ready to sign a check for an important program. It's a great thrill! It means that I've done something that is important. There's great joy in my giving. It's thrilling. It's exhilarating. It's important to be a part of sharing. It is my love. It is my joy."

> W. Clement Stone – Entrepreneur (Insurance), motivational speaker, philanthropist

"I love to do things for children because I get a kick out of it. Therefore, I am a selfish person and no philanthropist."

> W. K. Kellogg– Cereal magnate, philanthropist

"When I make a gift, I feel good all over. I actually glow. I love to give. I really enjoy giving. When you've got it, you're supposed to give it away. This is something I just feel inside me. And when I give, I look in the mirror and I think— wow, what a great thing I've done."

> Dorothy Simmerly– Major supporter of the Episcopal Church

All three quotes can be found in Jerold Panas' ancient (but still awesome) book titled "Mega Gifts" (originally published back in 1984). You can get it used for as low as 79 cents. It's worth every penny.

CHAPTER SEVEN:
Guest Posts and Other People

CHAPTER SEVEN - GUEST POSTS AND OTHER PEOPLE

3 MAJOR DONOR MYTHS BROKEN BY ANDREW OLSEN

Andrew Olsen knows a thing or two about direct marketing. On his blog, he debunks 3 major donor myths that pertain to marketing. You can find them below.

Myth #1: Major donors don't give through the mail or online

Myth #2: Your best donors will freak out if you contact them multiple times within a few months

Myth #3: Social service organizations (especially those that feed/shelter the homeless) don't have real major donor supporters

SMARTIDEAS: THE BEST OF 2017

ARE YOU HUNTING MICE OR ANTELOPES? (GUEST POST FROM T.J. MCGOVERN)

The following is a guest post thanks to my friend T.J. McGovern, Owner/Principal at McGovern Consulting Group (McG).

Here is a teaching story I usually share (with a tip of the hat to Tom Suddes):

A lioness can actually capture, kill and eat a field mouse.

However, it turns out that the energy burned doing that is greater than the caloric content of the mouse.

Therefore, if a lioness spends her whole day hunting and eating field mice … she would slowly starve itself to death! (Note: Lionesses do most of the hunting for the pride. The male lions stay home to watch the young cubs.)

A lioness cannot live on mice. She needs to eat antelopes. Antelopes are big.

Although antelopes require more speed and strength for the lioness to capture and kill them… once killed, they provide a huge feast for her, her cubs, her lion pal and the pride.

A lioness can live a long and happy life on a diet of antelope.

She will die "chasing mice".

If she spends all of her time and energy chasing "field mice," her short-term reward is a feeling of 'ACTIVITY', and maybe even a bit of 'ACCOMPLISHMENT'.

However, in the long run, without a doubt, she will die.

The lesson as it relates to fundraising is that each of us need to ask ourselves, "Are we spending our days CHASING MICE or HUNTING

CHAPTER SEVEN - GUEST POSTS AND OTHER PEOPLE

ANTELOPES? Do we even know the difference?"
"Do we know who our antelope are?"

"Are we going to continue doing special events (that aren't special), blasting spam, mailing junk, building awareness, rebranding and lord knows what else… mostly focused on 'MICE'?"

"Or are we going to make it essential that we focus all we've got on the ANTELOPES?"

RIDDLE: HOW DO YOU MEASURE THE SUCCESS (OR FAILURE) OF YOUR PLANNED GIVING PROGRAM? BY LIZZIE WEILAND

Today I'm very proud to provide a guest post written by one of MarketSmart's brilliant, yet curious, Account Managers—Lizzie Weiland. She's got an interesting riddle to solve. Let's see if you can help her figure it out.

It all started with what seemed to be a simple question.

I was speaking with a client recently about the success he's been experiencing with our software and strategies when he asked a really great question: **"How can I measure the success of my planned giving program in comparison to others?"**

He already knows that he's been discovering more "hidden" legacy gifts for his organization than ever before because he can easily compare past results with recent metrics. But he was wondering how his results compare to other nonprofits' figures because a board member was pressing him for a report.

At first he was hopeful that, perhaps, the answer could be boiled down to a simple benchmark formula such as — *Nonprofits should attain one new planned gift intention per year per 1,000 active donors.*

That sounded great! But it seemed way too good to be a true standard for performance.

Can this question be answered at all?

If you think about it for a minute, it's a real challenge. How exactly *ARE* fundraisers supposed to know how well *THEIR* planned giving program is doing compared to other nonprofits? How can they know if they are over-performing or under-performing? Does any simple metric exist?

I think it could be dangerous to compare one organization to another. After all, fundraisers always tell us that their organizations are different. Their donor lists are different. Their missions are different. And, their programs are different.

If that's the case, how can an "industry standard" exist for a planned giving program comparison metric?

I tried to figure it out anyway.

Of course, we couldn't tell him to just tell his board member, "It's tricky! Our organization is different!"

So, instead, I began to examine several factors in an attempt to normalize the data for a comparative analysis:
1. List size
2. Data integrity
3. Number of active donors versus inactive donors (or those who have never donated such as members or advocates)
4. The level of donor engagement with the organization

The plot thickens.

The more I thought about each of those factors, the more challenging this problem became.
1. **List size.** Each organization has a different number of records in their database. Some organizations have volunteers, members and advocates included while others only have donors. So should all the records be used as we calculate our number of legacy commitments per 1,000? Should that include volunteers, members, and advocates? Or just donors?
2. **Data integrity.** What if the data isn't good? That will affect the number of legacy commitments per 1,000 formula tremendously. For instance, was any part of the database purchased or appended? If so, should those records be included in the count? Did everyone in the database explicitly opt-in to the database? How did they get in there? Does the organization frequently remove unsubscribes, bounces, and bad mailing addresses to keep the list current? All of these factors impact the quality of a nonprofit's data.

3. **Active donors vs. inactive (or non-donors such as members or advocates).** If we decide to ignore the volunteers, members and advocates for our calculation, should we only look at active donors? I think doing so would be a big mistake. I've had several clients tell me that, more and more, they are receiving legacy gifts from people who never donated (non-donors). And in some cases, the number of legacy gifts from these non-donors is even higher than from their active donors. For instance, one of our clients receives 80% of their bequests from non-donors!
4. **Level of donor engagement with your organization.** Some organizations are very good at engaging donors and cultivating relationships while others ignore their donors or send them way too many asks via email. Since all this differs so tremendously for each organization, wouldn't it be safe to assume that highly engaged donors would be more likely to make a legacy gift? Alternatively, wouldn't we want to assume that organizations with low levels of donor engagement would generate fewer legacy gifts? If list size, data integrity and # of active vs. # of inactive donors are messy factors, should we focus on the # of engaged donors instead?

Very challenging isn't it?

Eureka! How about industry growth?

After thinking about the above factors, I got frustrated. So I started Googling the subject a bit and I think I might have found the answer thanks to a Blackbaud white paper. According to one of its authors (Katherine Swank— one of our pals!), **the best metric for determining how many legacy gift intentions you should be receiving each year** would have to be based on the industry growth as a whole for legacy gifts made each year.[10]

This seems to make a lot of sense.

---

10 https://www.blackbaud.com/files/resources/downloads/WhitePaper_ProspectResearchfor-PlannedGifts.pdf

CHAPTER SEVEN - GUEST POSTS AND OTHER PEOPLE

The report states that planned gifts to charitable organizations have grown on average 4.5% to 5% every year, even in economic downturns.

I think my client should use this formula with his own year-over-year data to determine how he's doing comparatively. For instance, if he received 40 intentions last year, then he should receive 42 next year (a 5% increase).

In other words, he probably should look solely at his program and how it is growing compared to the very simple industry growth percentage.

What do you think? Agree?

Do you have a formula you'd recommend?

THE 4 LEVELS OF DONOR COMMITMENT ACCORDING TO MAL WARWICK

For those of you who are new to the field, Mal Warwick played a tremendous leadership role in fundraising and direct marketing. In his book titled *How to Write Successful Fundraising Appeals*, he outlined the 4 levels of donor commitment. Here they are:

1. **The Tourist** – *No commitment:* These folks are not likely to give you money but they do respond to freebies and use your website to gather information. They *might* become donors if you give them enough value but it's doubtful.

2. **The Visitor** – *A bit of commitment:* They might be attracted to you in the same way the Tourist was but they become a bit more involved. They might subscribe to your e-newsletter or give a small donation.

3. **The Resident** – *A lot of commitment:* Residents aim to stick with you unless you screw it up. They have given on multiple occasions and could be monthly donors. They volunteer and attend events. Residents include former staff or board members too. All of these folks are great legacy gift prospects.

4. **The Lifer** – *The highest level of commitment:* Lifers are the residents that have stuck with your organization through thick and thin; good times and bad. Their undying passion makes them your best bet for legacy gifts.

How do your supporters fit into these personas? Are you overlooking some lifers?

CHAPTER SEVEN - GUEST POSTS AND OTHER PEOPLE

CLAIRE'S 9 WAYS TO GET THE MAJOR DONOR VISIT

Getting a donor to see you might actually be the hardest part of your job.

In fact, some fundraisers feel that, once they get the meeting set, they are 80% of the way there!

Thanks to Claire Axelrad, here's some help.

She's provided 9 useful, proven strategies for getting the major donor visit on her blog, which you can find here: https://clairification.com/2017/06/21/9-useful-proven-strategies-get-major-donor-visit/.

Here are my favorites (below) but you'll want to check out her blog for the rest:
1. Asking for advice.
2. Offer alternatives for the timing of the meeting.
3. Don't ask if you can drop by to tell them what your organization is doing.

I'd also add: Ask them about them, their needs, and their dreams.

WHY OPRAH WINFREY GIVES MONEY TO BUILD SCHOOLS IN AFRICA (THE 8 COMPONENTS OF IMPACTFUL GIVING)

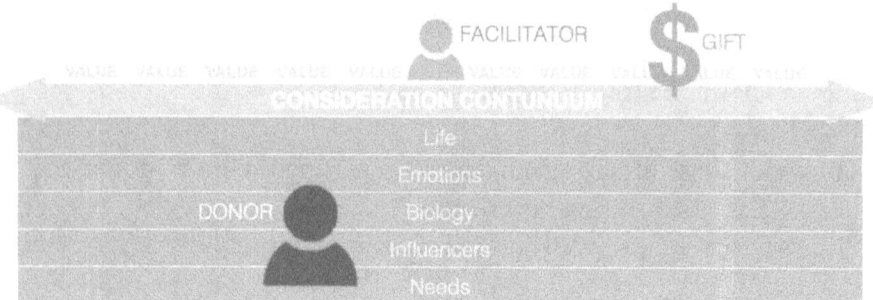

You might have known that Oprah was a philanthropist; but did you know why?

Most people think they know Oprah Winfrey, one of the richest self-made women in the world. Having survived rape and child molestation she became pregnant at the age of 14. Her son died in infancy and she began a career in radio. Now she is a media mogul, talk show host, actress, producer and billionaire. She is also a philanthropist.

In 2012, she was interviewed by Moira Forbes at the Forbes 400 Summit on Philanthropy. There she said, "True philanthropy comes from the heart." She went on to describe how poor she was growing up. Her grandmother only finished the third grade leading her to believe in education as her road to freedom.

She described the day her mother told her there would be no Christmas presents for her that year. She was sad and embarrassed. Not because she wouldn't get any presents. Rather, she was worried about what she'd tell her friends when they discussed what they got from Santa Claus.

CHAPTER SEVEN - GUEST POSTS AND OTHER PEOPLE

Here's when she became a philanthropist (but didn't know it yet)

Later that night, at around midnight, three nuns showed up at her door carrying baskets of food and toys for her and her half-sister and brother. They handed her a doll.

That's when she realized that people who didn't even know her name made sure she had a toy for Christmas. As a result, she felt a sense of relief because now she could tell her friends what she got. But she was also overtaken by a sense of wonder about the fact that people she didn't even know put forth the time and effort to figure out that her family needed food and toys.

Back to the interview with Moira Forbes

On-stage, with a sincere expression of both gratitude and admiration Oprah went on to say, "I never forgot that moment and years later, when I was contemplating how I wanted to use my own resources, I thought about those nuns. So my first venture was to go to South Africa to do for other children; to create that experience I felt for myself, that sense of wonder that somebody cared about me who didn't even know my name. I wanted to do that."

Here's her *WHY*

"I also knew what a *big role education had played in my life* and I always knew from the beginning of my success that I would have to find a way to *give back*. That's just part of *the way my grandmother raised me*; that to those whom much is given, much is expected. She never lived to see how much was given. But I was taught to give back."

The consideration process

So, next, Oprah expressed her interests in giving back with a focus on education in the media and soon she received an invitation to visit South Africa from Nelson Mandela. She stayed at his home for 10 days and 10 nights and toward the end of the visit, the two of them were sitting together reading the newspaper. By that time the two were very comfortable with one another and they got into a discussion about poverty and how to affect change. She told him *her story* along with *her WHY*.

Self-solicitation

Then Oprah proclaimed, "The only way to change poverty is through education and one day, I would like to build a school in South Africa."

After a brief pause, Nelson Mandella looked at Oprah and said, "You want to build a school?" Then he got up and called the Minister of Education. By that afternoon she was in a meeting talking about getting the project going.
That's how it works.

Oprah's impactful giving resulted from 8 major components.
1. Her life;
2. Her emotions;
3. Her biology;
4. Her influencers;
5. Her needs;
6. Her consideration continuum;
7. A value proposition;
8. And a facilitator (if you are a fundraiser… this is your role).

Let's review these components and Oprah's *WHY*

Oprah's *past life experiences* created memories.

When those memories were brought to the fore, she felt *emotions*.

Then her *biology* caused the release of certain chemicals in her brain.

The fact that the nuns were charitable to her and that her grandmother taught her to give back *influenced* her to want to reciprocate by helping others.

She began to realize that giving could provide a way for her personal *needs* to be met.

CHAPTER SEVEN - GUEST POSTS AND OTHER PEOPLE

Next, she sought out ways to *consider* how she might become more philanthropic.

Then she evaluated the *value* she and others would gain from her giving.

And, finally, she took action with a trusted *facilitator* with whom she built a relationship; on who shared her vision and could help make it a reality.

Your role
Your job is to figure out how to make this happen more often for your organization. But, if you are like most fundraisers, you don't have enough time or budget.

I promise, by understanding these components of impactful giving and by **leveraging technology** to provide value at every stage along the consideration continuum, you (the facilitator) *can* help those hi-capacity supporters (who feel aligned with your organization's mission) do what Oprah did in support of *your cause*.

7 GREAT OLD QUOTES ABOUT PHILANTHROPY

1. Abraham Lincoln famously said, "When I do good, I feel good; when I do bad, I feel bad; and that's my religion."
2. Booker T. Washington said, "If you want to lift yourself up, lift up someone else" and also said, "Those who are happiest are those who do the most for others."
3. Winston Churchill said, "We make a living by what we get. We make a life by what we give."
4. The Dalai Lama said, "If you want others to be happy, practice compassion. If you want to be happy, practice compassion."
5. Mark Twain said, "The best way to cheer yourself up is to try to cheer somebody else up."
6. Bob Hope said, "If you haven't got any charity in your heart, you have the worst kind of heart trouble."
7. And, Confucius said, "If you want happiness for a year, inherit a fortune. If you want happiness for a lifetime, help someone else."

ABOUT THE AUTHOR

In 2007 MarketSmart's founder, Greg Warner, received a newsletter from one of his beloved charities, which sought to generate leads for its planned giving department. He decided to call them to see if their impersonal, interruptive, mass-marketing approach was working well. It was not.

So, Greg decided to improve the effectiveness of the charity's lead generation and cultivation efforts with a fresh strategy. After implementing Greg's plan, the organization generated more highly qualified leads — and found more legacy gifts — than it had previously uncovered in any single marketing campaign, ever.

After that initial success, Greg recognized that the greatest transfer of wealth in U.S. history was imminent and decided to act. He realized that by combining his firm's understanding of technology with savvy marketing strategies and superior sales skills, MarketSmart could help nonprofit organizations increase the scale of their major gift and planned giving marketing efforts with greater efficiency. The firm's cornerstone engagement fundraising platform uses cutting-edge tracking technologies to help fundraisers zero-in on and effectively cultivate donors who are most likely to deliver large, major or legacy gifts.

www.ingramcontent.com/pod-product-compliance
Lightning Source LLC
Chambersburg PA
CBHW070151230526
45471CB00002B/619